Artisans Around the World

Mexico & Central America

Sharon Franklin, Mary Tull, and Cynthia A. Black

RSVP

RAINTREE
STECK-VAUGHN
P U B L I S H E R S
A Steck-Vaughn Company

Austin, Texas

www.steck-vaughn.com

Developed by Franklin Tull, Inc.,
Manager: Sharon Franklin
Designer: Dahna Solar
Maps: Terragraphics, Inc.
Illustrators: Dahna Solar and James Cloutier
Picture Researcher: Mary Tull
Projects: Cynthia A. Black

Raintree Steck-Vaughn Publishers Staff
Project Manager: Joyce Spicer
Editor: Pam Wells

Photo Credits: W.Bertsch/The Stock Solution: pp. 8UL, 8UR; Wm. Floyd Holdman/The Stock Solution: pp. 8LL, 24UR, 34LL, 35UR; CHOICE Humanitarian/Salt Lake City, Utah: pp. 8LR, 9L, 12UR; James Cloutier: pp. 11UL, 11C, 11L, 12C, 12CR, 12L, 38CR, 38LR; Peter Chartrand/D. Donne Bryant Stock Picture Agency: pp. 16UR, 16UL, 17UR, 17LR, 18L, 20UR; Michael Romanyshyn: pp. 16LL, 20L; John Mitchell/D. Donne Bryant Stock Picture Agency: pp. 16LR, 17LL, 18UR; Alyx Kellington/D. Donne Bryant Stock Picture Agency: p. 19UR; Ken Cole/The Stock Solution: pp. 24UL, 25UR, 25LR, 27UL, 28UL; Tom Zimberoff/The Stock Solution: pp. 24LL, 29UR; D. Donne Bryant/D. Donne Bryant Stock Picture Agency: p. 24LR; Tommy Dodson/Unicorn Stock Photos: p. 26L; Elizabeth Gibson: pp. 27CL, 30LR; Joel Sherzer: p. 28CR; Ann Petersen: pp. 29LL, 30LL; Anika Denali: pp. 34UL, 34UR, 36LL, 37CL, 39LL; Chris R. Sharp/D. Donne Bryant Stock Picture Agency: p. 34LR; Jelisa Peterson Zenzano: 35LL, 36UL, 38LL, 38UR. All project photos by James Cloutier.
[**Photo credit key:** First Letter: U-Upper; C-Center, L-Lower; Second letter: R-Right; L-Left]

Library of Congress Cataloging-in-Publication Data
Franklin, Sharon.
    Mexico and Central America / Sharon Franklin, Mary Tull, and Cynthia A. Black.
       p.   cm. — (Artisans around the world)
    Includes bibliographical references and index.
    Summary: Describes the cultures of Mexico, Nicaragua, Panama, and Guatemala and gives instructions
for projects that introduce local crafts of each country.
    ISBN 0-7398-0121-X
    1. Handicraft — Mexico — Juvenile literature. 2. Handicraft — Central America — Juvenile literature.
3. Mexico — Social life and customs — Juvenile literature. 4. Central America — Social life and customs —
Juvenile literature. [1. Handicraft — Mexico. 2. Handicraft — Central America. 3. Mexico — Social life and
customs. 4. Central America — Social life and customs.] I. Tull, Mary. II. Black, Cynthia A. III. Title. IV. Series.
TT28.F73   1999
745.5'0972 — dc21
                                                     98-49466
                                                  CIP   AC

Printed and bound in the United States
1 2 3 4 5 6 7 8 9 0 WO 03 02 01 00 99

Table of Contents

The icons next to the projects in the Table of Contents identify the easiest and the most challenging project in the book. This may help you decide which project to do first.

⇨ easiest project

✪ most challenging project

MEXICO

GUATEMALA

NICARAGUA

PANAMA

North
America

Central
America

South
America

N
W   E
S

0   500 miles

0   750 km

Introduction to Artisans Around the World

There are many ways to learn about the history and present-day life of people in other countries. In school, students often study the history of a country to learn about its people. In this series, you will learn about the history, geography, and the way of life of groups of people through their folk art. People who create folk art are called **artisans.** They are skilled in an art, a craft, or a trade. You will then have a chance to create your own folk art, using your own ideas and symbols.

What Is Folk Art?

Folk art is not considered "fine art." Unlike many fine artists, folk artisans do not generally go to school to learn how to do their art. Very few folk artists are known as "famous" outside of their countries or even their towns. Folk art is the art of everyday people of a region. In this series, folk art also includes primitive art, that is, the art of the first people to be in an area. But, beware! Do not let this fool you into thinking that folk art is not "real" art. As you will see, the quality of the folk art in this series is amazing by any standards.

Folk art comes from the heart and soul of common people. It is an expression of their feelings. Often, it shows their personal, political, or religious beliefs. It may also have a practical purpose or meet a specific need, such as the need for shelter. In many cases, the folk art in the "Artisans Around the World" series comes from groups of people who did not even have a word for art in their culture. Art was simply what people did. It was a part of being human.

Introduction to *Mexico and Central America*

In this book, you will learn about these crafts and the people who do them:

Tin ornaments in Mexico

Giant puppets in Nicaragua

Mola-making in Panama

Weaving in Guatemala

Then you will learn how to do projects of your own.

Here are some questions to think about as you read this book:

Did any of these folk arts help meet people's basic needs?

Which folk arts expressed people's religious, political, or personal views?

Were some of these folk arts traditionally created mostly by men or by women? Why do you think that was so? Is it still true today?

How did the history of a country influence some folk art traditions?

How did the geography, including the natural resources, of a country influence some folk art traditions? How did people get folk art materials that they needed but that were not found in their region?

Do some folk art traditions tell a story about a group of people or a culture? If so, in what way?

How have these folk art traditions been passed down from generation to generation?

Folk Art Today

Reading about these folk art traditions, as well as creating your own folk art,
will increase your respect for the people who first did them.
Do you think some of these art forms, such as *molas,*
could be created faster or more easily using machines, like the sewing machine,
or technology, like the computer? Do you think anything would be
lost by doing so, even if it were possible?

All of these folk art traditions of Mexico and Central America began long ago.
Can you think of any new folk art traditions being started now, in the
United States or in other countries? If so, what are they?
If not, why do you think there are no new traditions?

Safety Guidelines

These folk art projects are a lot of fun to do, but it's important to follow
basic safety rules as you work. Here are some guidelines to help as you
complete the projects in this book. Work slowly and carefully. That way
you can enjoy the process.

1. Part of being a responsible person of any age is knowing when to ask
   for help. Some of these projects are challenging. Ask an adult for help
   whenever you need it. Even where the book does not tell you to, feel
   free to ask for help if you need it.

2. Aluminum Safety
   • Ask an adult to work with you on the cutting.
   • Wear gloves while you cut the aluminum into workable sections.
   • Make long, smooth cuts so you don't leave any jagged edges.
   • Wrap masking tape around the edges of the aluminum before
     you work on it.

3. When painting, protect your clothing with an old shirt or a smock.
   When wet, acrylic paint can be removed with water. After it dries, it
   cannot be removed.

4. Handle all pointed tools, such as scissors, in a safe manner. Keep them
   stored in a safe place when not in use.

By the way, part of being an artist involves cleaning up! Be sure to clean up your work area
when you are finished. Also, remember to thank anyone who helped you.

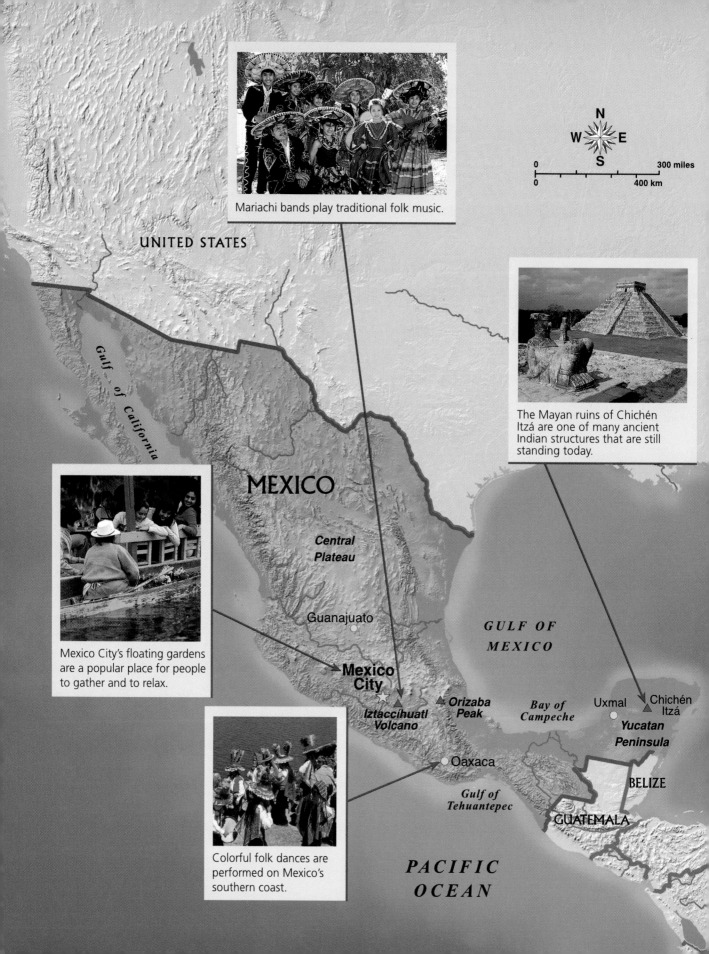

Mariachi bands play traditional folk music.

The Mayan ruins of Chichén Itzá are one of many ancient Indian structures that are still standing today.

UNITED STATES

Gulf of California

MEXICO

Central Plateau

Guanajuato

Mexico City

Iztaccihuatl Volcano

Orizaba Peak

GULF OF MEXICO

Bay of Campeche

Uxmal

Chichén Itzá

Yucatan Peninsula

Oaxaca

Gulf of Tehuantepec

BELIZE

GUATEMALA

PACIFIC OCEAN

Mexico City's floating gardens are a popular place for people to gather and to relax.

Colorful folk dances are performed on Mexico's southern coast.

N
W E
S

0   300 miles
0   400 km

Mexico

▲ Mexico City at night is a dazzling sight.

Mexico Facts

Name: Mexico (Estados Unidos Mexicanos, which means United Mexican States)
Capital: Mexico City
Borders: Pacific Ocean, Gulf of Mexico, Caribbean Sea, United States, Guatemala, Belize
Population: 97.5 million
Language: Official language: Spanish; over 50 different native languages are also spoken
Size: 758,136 sq. mi. (1,963,564 sq km)
High/Low Points: Orizaba Peak, 18,700 ft. (5,700 m); sea level along the 6,301-mile (10,142-km) coastline
Climate: Rainfall ranges from 4 in. (10 cm) per year on the Baja Peninsula to over 200 in. (508 cm) per year in the Chiapas Highlands of southern Mexico; extreme heat (over 110° F/43° C) in the lowlands; year-round frost on the high volcanic peaks
Wildlife: A rich variety of mammals, birds, reptiles, and amphibians. Unusual or rare species include the quetzal, jaguar, ocelot, harpy eagle, and Guadalupe fur seal
Plants: Wide variety of trees in forests, thousands of varieties of flowers, hundreds of cactus plants

A Blend of Past and Present

In Mexico tourists find large cities with skyscrapers, hotels, schools, museums, and other evidence of modern urban life. Just a short distance away, visitors can see ancient pyramids and small villages that have remained unchanged for centuries.

The majority of Mexicans are **mestizo.** A mestizo has both Indian and European ancestors. About one-quarter of Mexico's people belong to tribal communities that trace themselves back to ancient Indian cultures, including the Maya, Toltec, Mixtec, Zapotec, and Aztec. Many Indians live in small isolated villages. They raise their own food and make things by hand as their ancestors did. Some still speak ancient Indian languages.

▲ Mexico's highlands are full of mountain peaks and lush green valleys.

Mexico's Rugged Geography

More than one-half of Mexico's population lives in cities in the Central Plateau. This **plateau** runs through the center of Mexico from north to south. The western part of the plateau contains Mexico's most fertile valleys. Its many mountains hold enormous mineral wealth, but they are also volcanic and erupt from time to time. Throughout Mexico's history, the mountains have made transportation and communication difficult.

Roads now connect most parts of Mexico, but still, the crafts of each region often remain distinct, or different. In places like Guanajuato and Oaxaca, visitors can find many practical and artistic objects made from tin. Tin art has a new place in Mexico's long history of creating beautiful metalwork.

Aztec Empire

When Hernando Cortés and his men landed on the coast of Mexico in 1519, they heard stories of the great Aztec Empire. Greedy for gold and silver, Cortés carefully planned his assault on Tenochtitlán, the Aztec capital city. Imagine his delight when he entered the city and saw that the stories were all true. Tenochtitlán was as grand a city as any in Europe.

Long before the Spanish arrived, the early Indians of Mexico created masterpieces in gold, silver, and copper. Most jewelry and other items were made from gold. Nuggets and veins of gold were easily found, while silver had to be carefully removed from rocks.

Most of the fine gold and silver art created by Indian artisans was destroyed during the Spanish conquest. The Spanish wanted gold, not jewelry. They melted down the beautiful Indian jewelry and sent the metal home to Spain. This practice supplied Spanish artisans with raw materials, but it robbed Mexico of priceless pieces of art. Only a few objects, found in hidden places or in graves, still exist.

▲ Gold jewelry and other items, such as this gold mask of Xipe Totec, can be seen today in the Regional Museum in Oaxaca.

The Mixtec, Master Metalsmiths

The Mixtec people of the Oaxaca Highlands are considered the finest metalsmiths of ancient Mexico. They created beautiful jewelry, ornaments, and ceremonial objects for their temples. Mixtec gold jewelry and other items were found in the tombs of Mount Albán, near Oaxaca. Today, these items are displayed in the Regional Museum in Oaxaca.

Achievements of Mexico's Ancient Civilizations

Olmec: 1500 – 400 B.C.

- Mastery of stone carving
- Development of a counting system and calendar

Zapotec: 300 B.C.– A.D. 900

- First use of writing in this part of the world
- Construction of the pyramids at Mount Albán outside Oaxaca

Maya: A.D. 250 – 900

- Outstanding advances in mathematics and science
- Development of an accurate solar calendar
- Construction of tall limestone pyramids
- Development of hieroglyphics, an advanced form of writing

Mixtec: A.D. 692 – 1521

- Gold and silver artistry, stonework, carved wood and bone, and polychrome, or multicolored, pottery

Aztec: 1428 – 1521

- Identity as Mexico's mightiest empire
- Medical skill
- Composition of beautiful music and poetry

Tenochtitlán

The Aztecs built Tenochtitlán on an island in the middle of Lake Texcoco. They connected it to the mainland with roads and elevated ramps. The island was slowly extended with "floating gardens," soil taken from the lake's bottom. After conquering the Aztecs in the 1500s, the Spanish drained the lake. Today, Mexico City sits on top of the ruins of Tenochtitlán.

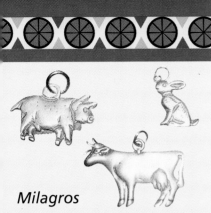

Milagros

When people pray for help, they may leave a *milagro* in the church as a gift or as a thank-you offering. *Milagros* are small, flat, two-inch pieces of gold or silver in the shapes of body parts or even animals. In some churches, the statues of saints are covered with tiny *milagros*.

Retablos

Retablos are small paintings on flattened tin. They include pictures, prayers, or words of thanks for prayers answered.

▲ Some *retablos,* like this one, were made a long time ago.

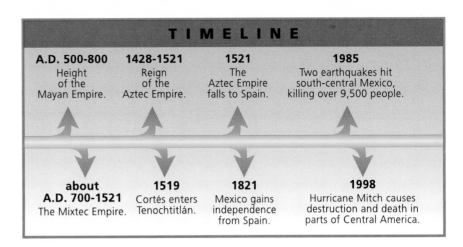

TIMELINE			
A.D. 500-800 Height of the Mayan Empire.	**1428-1521** Reign of the Aztec Empire.	**1521** The Aztec Empire falls to Spain.	**1985** Two earthquakes hit south-central Mexico, killing over 9,500 people.
about A.D. 700-1521 The Mixtec Empire.	**1519** Cortés enters Tenochtitlán.	**1821** Mexico gains independence from Spain.	**1998** Hurricane Mitch causes destruction and death in parts of Central America.

The Introduction of Tin

The Spaniards quickly **exploited** Mexico's mineral wealth. They dug mines to extract gold, silver, iron, tin, and copper from the land. They also forced the Indians to work as slaves in the mines in Mexico's deserted north country. Many Indians died there, far from their highland homes.

Iron, steel, and tin were unknown to the ancient peoples of Mexico. The Spanish taught Indians the skills and techniques necessary to make iron and tin ready for use. After the Spanish conquest, the Indians were forbidden to possess gold, silver, or any other valuable metal. Because the Spaniards had outlawed the use of precious metals, the Indians turned to tin.

Today, candlesticks, jewelry, mirror frames, and trays are made from tin, just as they were after the Spanish conquest. You can see exotic and practical metalwork, including tin, in Guanajuato. Rich veins of silver were discovered in nearby mountains during the 16th century. This made Guanajuato the cultural center of Mexico for many years.

You can also find tin art in the charming tourist city of Oaxaca. Oaxaca city reflects the culture of Indian Mexico. The state of Oaxaca has the largest native Indian population of any Mexican state. In the *mercados,* or markets, you can purchase shiny hammered copper cooking pots, brass goblets, and tile-topped iron tables, along with many colorful and inexpensive things made of tin.

Tin

Tin is a white, metallic element used in the production of tin plate. Tin plate is steel coated on both sides with a thin film of tin. Tin protects the steel from rusting and makes the object more attractive. Most tin plate is made into tin cans.

Tin Art

Folk art is popular with tourists and Mexicans alike. Shoppers can choose from tin work, black pottery, and handloomed rugs. There are wood carvings, woven baskets, and many other creations. Some are traditional handicrafts. Other designs use traditional skills in new and exciting ways.

Many Mexican artists today use tin because it is readily available and inexpensive. Tin is also light and flexible. It bends into place and can be cut, hammered, and punched to create almost any design imaginable. Artists use tin to craft tiny candleholders, lanterns, serving trays, toys, Christmas ornaments, and many other items. They may be decorated with brass or copper, or painted in bright colors. Oaxacan artist Aarón Velasco Pacheco cuts fanciful and colorful figures such as giraffes, horses, pigs, butterflies, and even skeletons out of thin sheets of tin.

▲ Traditional folk dancers wear tin headpieces that reflect the rich colors in their costumes.

Almost any animal or object can be ▲ made into a colorful tin ornament.

▲ Some tin objects are decorated with gold.

Art from Recycled Material

Tin work is often a craft of the Mexican poor. They are masters of recycling. Nothing is thrown away if it can serve a useful purpose. Recycling old tin objects and turning them into something new excites the imagination! Families add to their incomes by creating colorful and useful things out of tin cans.

Discarded oil and milk cans are used to make decorative spiral, fan, and shell stamps for the tops of *pan dulce* (a Mexican sweet bread).

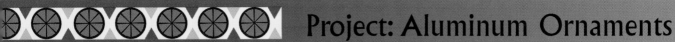
Tools

- old pair of scissors
- stamping and piercing tools (blunt-tipped stick, nail, bolt, screwdriver)
- embossing tools (paintbrush handle, spoon, wooden clay modeling tools)
- pencil
- awl or heavy needle

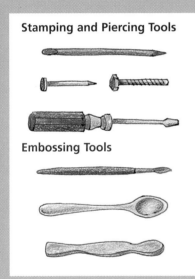

Stamping and Piercing Tools

Embossing Tools

Materials

- disposable aluminum pie plates or cookie sheets, available in grocery stores—look for ones with a smooth surface and few words or patterns
- masking tape
- newspapers
- paper
- permanent markers in bright colors
- string or yarn

Working with thin sheets of aluminum is easier and safer than working with tin. You can use the same decorating techniques that Mexican tin artists use for their ornaments.

Prepare the Aluminum

Tin can be a dangerous metal to cut and to handle because of its sharp edges. You can get similar results with thin pieces of sheet aluminum. The tools and techniques are a little different, because aluminum is a much softer metal. Follow the safety guidelines as you prepare the aluminum.

1. Use scissors to cut off the side edges of the pie plate or cookie sheet. Use an old pair, though, because cutting aluminum will dull the blades. **Ask an adult to work with you on the cutting.** *(See diagram.)*

2. Cut out several small sections of flat aluminum. Wrap masking tape around the edges. *(See diagram.)*

Aluminum Safety

- Wear gloves while you cut the aluminum into workable sections.
- Make long, smooth cuts so you don't leave any jagged edges.
- Wrap masking tape around the edges of the aluminum before you work on it.

Prepare the Aluminum

1. Cut off the side edges.

2. Cut out sections. Wrap edges.

Experiment with embossing and stamping the
▼ aluminum before you make an ornament.

Experiment With Aluminum

Aluminum has many possibilities. Take time to experiment before you make a finished ornament. Spread out a thick layer of newspapers to work on for smooth, cushioned support. Try out the different techniques and tools.

Stamping and Piercing

In Mexico, *stamping* is often used to decorate metal. Patterns are pressed into tin with tools of different shapes.

1. Experiment with stamping. Use a blunt-tipped stick or a paintbrush handle to draw lines. Make dots by gently pressing a nail into the aluminum. Make other shapes and patterns with the tools you have collected. Find out what is possible, and how much pressure you can use. *(See diagram.)*

2. Also try stamping all the way through the aluminum, leaving a hole. This is called *piercing. (See diagram.)*

Embossing

In *embossing,* a design is pushed out, little by little, with a special blunt-tipped tool. Embossing gives a flat piece of metal some depth. Embossing can be either raised or sunken.

1. On another piece of aluminum, experiment with embossing. Use a blunt-tipped stick to draw the outline of a simple design. *(See diagram.)*

2. Here's how to emboss some areas of the design so they are raised. Flip the aluminum over to the back side. Trace a second outline on the inside edge of the first outline. *(See diagram.)*

3. Rub inside these areas with a wider tool, such as a clay modeling tool or a fat paintbrush handle. Smooth and stretch the aluminum so that it begins to swell out. *(See diagram.)*

4. Now follow these steps to emboss other areas of the design so that they are sunken. Flip the aluminum over to the front again. Trace a second outline as before. Rub the areas to push them to the back side. *(See diagram.)*

5. Go from front to back, gradually stretching the aluminum further and further. Experiment with how far you can push the metal before it gets too thin. Don't worry if it tears. This is just a test!

Stamping and Piercing

1-2. Experiment with stamping and piercing.

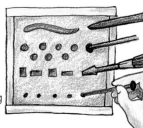

lines

dots

other shapes

piercing

Embossing

1. Draw the outline.

2. Trace a second outline.

3. Rub the raised areas.

4. Rub the sunken areas.

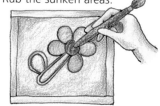

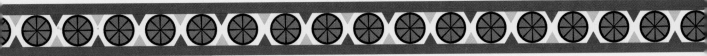

2. Trace over all of the lines.

3. Stamp and emboss.

4. Cut out the shape. Fold edges to the back.

Make an Ornament

As you design your ornament, consider the possibilities for stamping and embossing. Look over your experiments. Notice the way the light reflects off the surface of the metal and how shadows form in the sunken places. It is this quality that makes tin ornaments so eye-catching.

1. Draw a pattern for your ornament on paper. Make it large enough so that you have a good-sized area to work on. Plan the lines and shapes you will stamp or emboss. They can be decorative patterns or details, like feathers or facial features. Decide which areas will be raised and which will be sunken.

2. Lay your pattern on top of a piece of aluminum. Trace over all the lines lightly with a blunt-tipped stick to transfer the design. (Remember to work on a pad of newspapers.) Remove the pattern. *(See diagram.)*

3. Stamp and emboss the ornament as you planned. Leave some areas undecorated for contrast. *(See diagram.)*

4. Cut out the shape of the ornament with scissors. If you want, you can fold the edges to the back. This will help to make your ornament stronger. *(See diagram.)*

5. Color the ornament with permanent markers. Let the colored ink dry before you handle the ornament, or it will smudge.

6. Poke a small hole in the top of your ornament with an awl or a heavy needle. Thread a piece of string through the hole and tie it so you can hang the ornament.

Students' finished ▶ aluminum ornaments.

Other Ideas

■ Design a toy animal made out of aluminum.

■ Emboss and stamp a large piece of aluminum for a picture frame. Glue it onto a picture mat. Cut tabs to fold around the edges.

CARIBBEAN SEA

Gulf of Honduras

Momotombo is one of many volcanoes in Nicaragua.

HONDURAS

Mosquito Coast

Folk musicians sing songs that tell of the achievements and struggles of Nicaraguan people.

▲ *Mogotón Peak*

Coco River

Cordillera Isabelia

Matagalpa River

Gulf of Fonseca

Casita Volcano ▲
León

Lake Managua

NICARAGUA

Momotombo Volcano
★ Managua   ○ Masaya

Several large islands lie in Lake Nicaragua. The largest island has two volcanoes.

PACIFIC OCEAN

Lake Nicaragua

CARIBBEAN SEA

COSTA RICA

Puppets and performers on stilts are an important part of Nicaraguan street performances.

N
W E
S

| 0 | | 75 miles |
| 0 | | 100 km |

Nicaragua

Nicaragua Facts

Name: Republic of Nicaragua (República de Nicaragua)
Capital: Managua
Borders: Honduras, Costa Rica, Pacific Ocean, Caribbean Sea
Population: 4,400,000
Language: Official language: Spanish; main Native Indian language spoken: Miskito; English spoken in the Caribbean lowlands area
Size: Largest country in Central America; 50,200 sq. mi. (130,000 sq km)
High/Low Points: Mogotón Peak, 6,913 ft. (2,107 m); sea level along the coast
Climate: Tropical; 86° F (30° C) in lowlands to below 59° F (15° C) in mountains at night. Annual rainfall averages 70 inches (178 cm), but some parts of the Caribbean region get over 200 inches (508 cm)
Wildlife: 700 species of birds; over 200 species of mammals and fish; 300 species of reptiles and amphibians
Plants: About 7,000 different types, including 1,000 types of orchids
Volcanoes: Around 40 volcanoes, about 12 of which are active

From Managua to León

On a two-hour bus trip through the Pacific region of Nicaragua, visitors can witness the beauty and history of Central America's largest country. The bus departs from Managua, Nicaragua's present-day capital and largest city. Then it heads northwest to León, the country's first capital, which was moved to its present location in 1610.

▲ Managua is the bustling capital of the largest country in Central America.

During the trip, travelers view Momotombo, a volcano rising majestically into the clouds. It is one of 27 volcanoes along Nicaragua's Pacific Coast. Nicaragua is located on the Ring of Fire, a narrow belt that runs along the edges of the continents and the islands surrounding the Pacific Ocean. This area contains the most intense earthquakes and volcanoes in the world.

Throughout its history, Nicaragua has suffered devastating earthquakes and fires. In 1998, Hurricane Mitch left over 4,000 people dead or missing and over half a million people homeless. At the height of the storm, a slope of Casita volcano came crashing down. The mud buried four villages at the base of the mountain.

Evidence of the country's political struggles and civil wars is everywhere. Bullet holes in buildings, political murals on walls, and poor living conditions for many people are the results of the political violence that Nicaraguan people have endured for generations. Today, the armed fighting has stopped. Once ruled by a **dictator,** Nicaraguans now elect a president every six years. Nicaraguans are working hard to rebuild their country.

Soon the bus arrives in León, an historic city where Nicaraguans use art and theater to lift their spirits and defend their rights.

◀ Murals remind Nicaraguans of their history and political struggles.

Destructive ▶ earthquakes have caused Nicaragua's people great suffering.

350 B.C.-A.D. 300
Earliest evidence of human occupation.

1838
Nicaragua becomes an independent republic.

1937
The Somoza rule of dictators begins.

1980s
Contra war against the Sandinista regime.

1998
Hurricane Mitch hits Nicaragua, leaving 4,000 dead or missing and half a milion people homeless.

1500s-1821
The Spanish conquest and rule.

1912-1923 1927-1933
The U.S. Marines occupy Nicaragua.

1979
Sandinistas overthrow Somoza government.

1990
Violeta Barrios de Chamorro elected president.

1997
Arnoldo Alemán Lacayo becomes president.

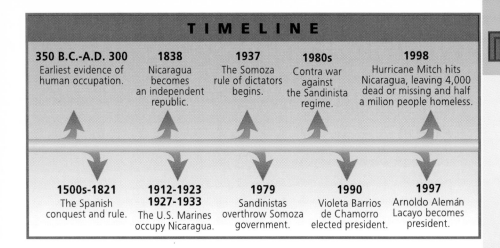

▲ León's beautiful cathedral is the largest church in Central America.

Subtiava

León is a beautiful and colorful city with houses roofed in red tile. Many neighborhoods have cobblestone streets and buildings that date from Spanish colonial times. One neighborhood, called Subtiava, is the home of the area's Indian artisans.

Conquest and Resistance

In 1502, on his fourth and final trip to the New World, Christopher Columbus sailed to Nicaragua and claimed it for Spain. By 1609 León had become the capital of the Spanish colonial government. The Indian peoples were conquered, and Spanish rule was established. León was the major city and trading center. It was also the center of the Roman Catholic church. León's gleaming white cathedral, which took 100 years to build, is still the largest church in Central America.

Throughout its history, Nicaragua has been ruled by dictators and occupied by foreign armies. Its people have suffered from poverty, fear, and political **oppression.** León became the center of **resistance,** where people fought against the government. Today, the bullet holes in the walls of León's University of Nicaragua are reminders of the fighting that took place in 1979. This was when the Sandinistas ended the Somoza dictatorship.

Somoza dictatorship
The Somoza family ruled Nicaragua for 42 years, from 1937 to 1979. They maintained firm control over the country's activities. They held most of the country's assets, while most of the Nicaraguan people lived in fear and poverty.

Sandinistas
Rebels who fought against the Somoza dictatorship and overthrew the government in 1979.

After the Sandinistas came to power in 1979, the fledgling government needed lots of help to shore up its economy in the world market. This mural shows the Sandinistas picking Nicaragua's most important crop – coffee.

Art for the People

The Nicaraguan people have a strong tradition of self-expression through poetry, painting, music, and theater. Nicaraguans have used art to voice their suffering, their anger, their political opinions, and their hopes for a better world.

▲ Nicaraguan muralists paint scenes that represent their daily life and culture.

In recent decades, plays in the street have been performed in war zones. Actors from the National Theater Workshop live among the local people to learn about their struggles. They write and perform plays that speak directly to people's experiences. Murals are also created that express political messages or tell stories of historical events.

The *Gigantona:* The Giant One

In Subtiava and elsewhere throughout Nicaragua, a centuries-old Indian tradition continues in performances of the *gigantona.* As musicians play, this richly decorated eight-foot puppet dances in the streets with her sidekick, the little Pepe. Crowds of people follow her as she twirls and swings through the street. Pepe recites ballads, tells jokes, and teases the crowd with witty remarks.

The *gigantona* was first used by the Indians in León to make fun of their Spanish colonial masters. In these early times, the *gigantona's* eyes were lit with candles. Often appearing at night, the *gigantona* and Pepe would dance through the streets. They told stories that spoke of independence and encouraged the people to resist the government.

◀ The *gigantona* has traditionally performed with traveling street theater groups. These groups present plays and political humor in cities and country villages.

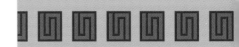

A Tool for Revolution

The *gigantona's* performances were very important during the war between the Somoza government and the Sandinista revolutionaries in the 1970s. The *gigantona* and Pepe were brought to demonstrations held to free political prisoners held by Somoza's National Guard. Pepe recited political verses that described the unfair treatment of prisoners. The puppets were also taken to the homes of people who were suspected of supporting Somoza. There, the *gigantona* danced, and Pepe read poems accusing those people of being against the revolution.

Gigantona Artisans and Performers

Visitors to Nicaragua will probably see a performance of the *gigantona*. It is common to see her dance on market days to entertain tourists. The *gigantonas* are created and performed by groups of street artists in various cities. Artisans create the puppet with papier-mâché and wood. A dancer slides under the puppet's clothing and climbs up on **stilts** to walk and dance. These artisans are responsible for keeping alive the *gigantona* tradition.

Nicaraguan Festivals

Throughout the year, the *gigantona* is part of Nicaragua's rich festival tradition that includes parades, religious ceremonies, music, and dancing. One of the largest festivals is the Festival of Disguises, a carnival held in Masaya. People dress up in fancy costumes to attend parades, dances, and banquets. Behind the protection of a mask, people can voice their beliefs and dress and act as they please. Like the *gigantona*, Nicaraguans in disguise express their opinions with passion and humor.

▲ This memorial in Managua honors Rubén Darío, Nicaragua's most famous poet.

A Nation of Poets

Almost everyone in Nicaragua writes poetry. Poems are another way for Nicaraguans to express their struggles, fears, and hopes. Nicaragua has produced more poets than any other Latin American country. Its most famous poet, Rubén Darío, is buried in León's cathedral.

At yearly festivals ▶ Nicaraguans often use oversized masks to poke fun at both famous and local characters.

Head Materials

- long cardboard tube
- masking tape
- duct or strapping tape
- newspapers
- large brown paper grocery bag
- pieces of thin cardboard
- papier-mâché paste
- white or brown latex enamel paint
- acrylic paints
- paintbrushes
- yarn or other materials for hair (optional)

Body Materials

- light bamboo pole, 4 ft. (1.2 m) long
- 1 thin strip of wood, 3 ft. (1 m) long
- piece of polyurethane foam, 3 ft. by 1 ft. (1 m by 30 cm)
- skin-toned fabric or large work gloves
- needle and thread
- fiberfill or other stuffing
- costume materials (a very large old shirt or dress; lightweight fabric, such as an old sheet)
- netting, lace, or fringe for a view hole
- 2 bamboo garden stakes

This dramatic figure is good to make together with a few friends. It is impressive, and surprisingly easy to construct.

Plan Your Giant Puppet

The *gigantona* is traditionally a giant lady, but your puppet can be anyone you wish. Think about making your favorite hero or a giant self-portrait. To begin, draw a picture of your puppet's head. Show a front and side view. Remember, this is a GIANT puppet. The facial features should be exaggerated so they can be seen from a distance.

Search in thrift stores and at yard or garage sales for clothes for your puppet. They need to be very large, with loose armholes. You can also sew a simple costume from an old sheet. Plan for a puppet that is about 2 feet (60 cm) taller than you are.

Make the Head Form

1. Use a long cardboard tube to make the puppet's neck. Block one end of the tube with a wad of newspaper. Cover that end with a piece of strong duct tape.

2. Fill the large paper bag partway with crumpled newspapers. Put the taped end of the tube into the center of the bag. Add more newspapers until the tube is held firmly in place. Push the papers down. Gather the open end of the bag tightly around the tube. The bag should feel very firm.

3. Wrap duct tape around the gathered edges of the bag. Cut the tube off so that it extends 4 inches (10 cm) out from the bag. *(See diagram.)*

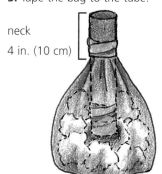

Make the Head Form

3. Tape the bag to the tube.

neck

4 in. (10 cm)

4. Mold the paper bag with your hands until the head looks round. Squash down the boxy corners. Use plenty of masking tape to help retain the shape. Wrap newspapers around the neck to build it up, and tape them firmly in place. Mold and tape the chin and the eye sockets.

5. Make a large nose with a large triangle of thin cardboard folded in half. Cut large cardboard ears. Tape the ears and nose in place. Make changes until the face looks right and the surfaces are smooth.

Papier-mâché the Head

Puppet ▶
head form.

1. Cover a table with a plastic tablecloth or a garbage bag. Mix the papier-mâché paste and paper pulp. Tear some newspaper into strips.

2. Dip the newspaper strips into the paste. Cover the head with one layer of strips. Use a generous amount of paste. Cover the nose, chin, neck, and partway down the sides of the head. Don't paper the back of the head.

3. Use the paper pulp to make eyebrows, cheeks, and lips. Use flat strips of newspaper dipped in paste to improve the shape of the nose and chin. To make eyes, roll balls of pulp and set them into the eye sockets. Cover them at the top and bottom with newspaper eyelids. *(See diagram.)*

4. Cover the entire face with two or three more layers of strips. Cover over all the features made with pulp to help hold them in place. If the surface begins to look very pasty, apply some dry strips to soak up the excess. Smooth the surface as much as possible.

5. The head will take from three days to one week to dry. When it is dry and hard, brush the whole head with enamel paint. This will cover the newspaper ink. It will also help to make the head stronger. **When painting, protect your clothing with an old shirt or a smock. When wet, acrylic paint can be removed with water. After it dries, it cannot be removed.**

6. Mix a skin-tone color with acrylic paints and cover the face and head. When the skin color is dry, paint the lips, eyes, and cheeks. Add yarn, crepe paper, or strips of fabric for the hair.

Build the Body Structure

1. Slip the pole into the neck tube so that the end nestles into the wad of newspapers. Make a mark on the pole at the end of the tube. Remove the head. *(See diagram.)*

Papier-mâché the Head

3. Form parts of the face.

eyebrows
eyelids
eyes
cheeks
lips

Build the Body Structure

1. Slip the pole into the neck tube.

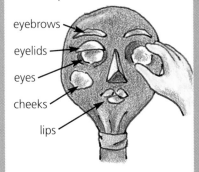

mark here ➞
bamboo pole ➞

22

2. Attach the shoulder crosspiece.

shoulder
crosspiece

3. Slide the foam over the pole.

Finish Your Puppet

2. Add hands.

3. Climb inside your puppet.

4. Cut a view hole.

2. Now make the shoulder crosspiece. Cut the thin wood strip to fit the shoulder width of the puppet's costume. Center the strip just below the mark on the pole. Use duct tape to attach the strip to the pole. The tube should rest on the wood strip when the head is in place. *(See diagram.)*

3. Cut a hole in the exact center of the polyurethane foam. Make the hole just big enough for the neck tube to fit through snugly. Slide the foam over the pole and bend it around the shoulder crosspiece. Wrap tape around the foam to shape the shoulders. The foam should stand out enough to make the costume look full. *(See diagram.)*

Finish Your Puppet

1. Dress the puppet in a large dress or shirt. For pants, cut two slits in a sheet and pin it together at the ankles.

2. Cut out two pairs of large hands from fabric. Sew each pair together. (Or use work gloves instead.) Stuff the hands and sew them to the bottom of the sleeves. To control your puppet's arms, insert bamboo stakes under the costume and into the hands. For a simpler puppet, let the arms dangle. *(See diagram.)*

3. Put the head in place. Climb inside your puppet with the pole in front of you. Rest the end of the pole on a sash or wide belt tied around your waist. Strap the pole around your chest. *(See diagram.)*

4. Cut a view hole in the costume at eye level and disguise it with lace, netting, or fringe. *(See diagram.)*

Other Ideas

■ You can attach the pole to the back of an old backpack frame. This allows complete hand freedom.

Presenting the ▶ finished *gigantonas*!

Ships from all nations pass through the Panama Canal. A system of locks raises ships from sea level to almost 85 feet above sea level and back down again.

The San Blas Islands are full of exotic birds. The Kuna make pets of some wild birds, and small children may walk around with birds on their heads or shoulders.

ATLANTIC OCEAN

CARIBBEAN SEA

COSTA RICA

N
W E
S

0   75 miles
0   100 km

Panama Canal

Colón

Panama City

San Blas Islands

Mosquito Gulf

Lake Bayano

Bayano R.

Barú Volcano

PANAMA

Bay of Panama

Darién Gap Region

Pan - American Highway

Rey Island

Yaviza

Gulf of Panama

Coiba Island

Azuero Peninsula

COLOMBIA

PACIFIC OCEAN

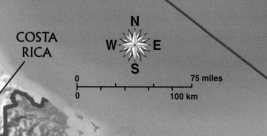

Panama City has ancient buildings alongside modern office buildings and apartments. The Bridge of the Americas connects the city to the west side of the Panama Canal.

The Panama rain forest has many species of rare plants and animals.

Panama

▲ *Ulus* are prized possessions. They are used for fishing, trips to the mainland, and for transport between islands.

Panama Facts

Name: Republic of Panama (República de Panamá); "The Bridge of the World"
Capital: Panama City
Borders: Caribbean Sea, Pacific Ocean, Costa Rica, and Colombia
Population: Panama: 2.7 million people; one-half within the Canal Zone region; San Blas: 28,567 in 54 communities
Language: Official language: Spanish; nearly one-half Kuna population bilingual in the Kuna language and Spanish
Size: 29,762 sq. mi. (77,082 sq km); rarely exceeds width of 75 mi. (120 km)
High/Low Points: Barú volcano: 11,400 ft. (3,475 m); sea level along coasts
Climate: Tropical, hot, humid; temperatures range between 71° F (22° C) and 87° F (31° C); rainy season: May-December
Wildlife: Highest diversity in bird, mammal, and amphibian species in Central America; many unusual animal species found nowhere else
Plants: Mahogany forests, dense jungle, palm trees, banana plants

Arriving in Panama

From the airplane window, low mountains can be seen running the length of Panama's narrow mainland like a jagged backbone. The highest point is Barú volcano, an extinct volcano rising 11,400 ft. (3,475 m) in the air. The mountains gradually slope down, reaching sea level on Panama's coasts. The big plane descends through a layer of puffy clouds and lands at an airport outside of Panama City. The air is thick and hot.

At the airport, visitors hop into a small yellow plane for a short flight out to the coast. A grassy runway opens up a few feet from the sea. An *ulu*, a traditional dugout canoe now powered with an outboard motor, carries passengers out to one of the San Blas Islands, about 15 minutes away.

The San Blas Islands and the Kuna Indians

The largest group of Kuna Indians resides on the San Blas Islands, which they refer to as Kuna Yala. The San Blas are a long, narrow strip of mainland jungle and an **archipelago** of several hundred small islands along Panama's Caribbean coast. Since about 1880, Kuna women have created *molas*, a creative style of needlework found nowhere else on earth. *Mola* means "clothing," "dress," or "blouse" in Kuna language. *Mola* also refers to the stitched panel of a Kuna woman's blouse. *Molas* feature vibrant color combinations and intricate patterns that record every aspect of Kuna life, culture, and history.

Kuna Indians

There are four groups of Kuna Indians. The vast majority of Kuna live in the San Blas Islands.

■ The San Blas Kuna inhabit 52 of the San Blas Islands and several coastal villages.

■ The Kuna Brave live in the center of the Darién jungle.

■ The Bayano Kuna live in villages on the Bayano River.

■ The Colombian Kuna live in villages across the Colombian border.

Kuna artists display ▶ their blouses by hanging them on lines for tourists to see.

The Spanish Arrive

When Spanish explorer Rodrigo de Bastidas reached what is now Panama in 1502, over 200,000 native peoples were living there. The Spanish, attracted by gold in the region, claimed this area for Spain. They tortured and killed all but a small number of the Kuna, Guaymí, and Chocó peoples and established settlements on their land. Many other native people died later from European diseases or from slave conditions in the gold mines. Kuna survivors retreated to the remote San Blas Islands and deeper into the mountain jungles of the Darién Gap where the invaders could not follow.

How the Kuna Survived

The Kuna Indians who fled were largely left alone. They are one of very few Latin American groups never conquered by the Spanish. In 1925, years of cruel treatment by the Panamanian government led to a Kuna revolt. As a result, the government recognized Kuna independence and the right of Kuna people to a traditional way of life. In 1930, the Kuna gained the right to be self-governing. They got the land known as Kuna territory, a narrow strip of land along Panama's northeast coast and the nearby San Blas Islands. A governor lives on one of the islands. He is the link between the village Kuna chiefs, or *saylas,* and the Panamanian government. In 1972, the Kuna elected three representatives to Panama's legislature, giving them an official voice in national politics. It is a role they take very seriously.

The Kuna's remote geographical location has helped them to survive and to maintain their own individual culture. They have retained a most unusual and original democracy.

Nele Kantule

Kuna revolutionary leader Nele Kantule played a major role in Kuna independence. Kantule viewed forced **assimilation,** the joining or mixing with other groups, as damaging to the Kuna way of life.

Bridge of the World

Over 60 million years ago, the Pacific Ocean floor began to divide. A ridge emerged out of the sea. Over millions of years, it became an **isthmus** dividing the Pacific and Atlantic oceans. This narrow strip of land is Panama. The Spaniards built a stone road across it to transport Inca treasures to the Atlantic coast. In 1848, gold seekers from the Eastern United States sailed to Panama, crossed the isthmus to the Pacific, and sailed north to California. There they joined in the gold rush. The Panama Canal, built across the isthmus, changed trade routes for all time.

Panama Canal

The canal provided a 50-mile-long route for ships across the narrowest part of Panama. Before that time, ships were forced to travel around the tip of South America in order to sail between the Pacific and Atlantic oceans. Panama's two largest cities, Panama City and Colón, are located at opposite ends of the canal.

The Darién Gap

Few tourists or Panamanians visit the Darién Gap. This region includes the mountainous area southeast of Lake Bayano down to the Colombia border. Most of this rain forest jungle can be reached only by boat or canoe. Then a **machete** is needed to cut through the thick jungle. The Pan-American Highway, which extends from the U.S.-Mexican border to the southern tip of Chile, stops in the jungle at Yaviza. It begins again about 90 miles (140 km) farther south across the Colombia border. This region of rain forest provides a buffer, or protective area, between Colombia and Panama to help prevent diseases carried by cattle from spreading into Panama.

Saving the Rain Forest

Over 200 species of animals inhabit the rain forest, including tapirs, golden harlequin toads, white-faced capuchin monkeys, and other unusual wildlife. In order to protect the rain forest, the Kuna created their own rain forest reserve. The Kuna Wildlife Project enables scientists from around the world to study the rain forest.

▲ Scientists come from all over the world to study the plants and animals of Panama's rain forest.

Kuna History, Geography, and Culture in Walking Pictures

The birds, animals, plants, and insects of Panama have all been carefully stitched into *molas*. Even historical events, inventions, and movie posters were used in *mola* designs. In the early 1900s, Kuna men worked in the Canal Zone to help build the Panama Canal. They saw many interesting new objects and brought some of them home. They were included in new *mola* designs. *Molas* created during World War II contained images of the American flag, Army posters, and airplanes. Baseball and basketball *molas* appeared after the war.

TIMELINE

Early 16th century	1903	1925	1972	2000
The Spanish arrive.	Panama gains independence from Colombia and signs the canal agreement with the U.S.	Kuna revolt and declare San Blas an "independent republic."	Kuna elect three representatives to the legislature.	U.S. scheduled to transfer complete control of the canal to Panama.

60 million years ago	1821	1914	1930	1989
A ridge emerges out of the sea and becomes an isthmus dividing the Pacific and Atlantic oceans.	Panama is liberated from Spain and becomes part of Colombia.	The Panama Canal opens.	The Kuna gain the right to govern themselves.	U.S. invades Panama in an attempt to capture General Manuel Noreiga.

▲ In a Kuna village one house is used for sleeping. Another house is used for preparing food and eating.

A Day in the Life

Most Kuna Indians still live in one-room huts. Eight or ten **extended family** members sleep in individual hammocks strung in a row across the room. Getting fresh water is often the first chore of the day, along with washing clothes, gathering firewood, and tending crops. Men may work with their boats or travel to other islands on business. When the afternoon sun is hot, it is *siesta,* or rest, time. Later, children swim or play games, while teenagers study or play basketball. Kuna families spend hours talking to and playing with their children.

Kuna Houses

Kuna houses have sturdy frames made from tree branches and walls made of bamboo stakes. The roofs are covered with thatch from palm trees. Thatch keeps the houses cool and dim during the hot days and protects against cool nights.

The *Congreso*

At nightly meetings, called the *congreso,* important issues are discussed and decisions are made. Disputes are discussed and resolved by **consensus.** The Kuna keep their history and traditions alive through chanted tales and songs, since they have no written language. The women listen as they sew. They talk about the meaning of the stories in everyday life.

▲ Chief Muristo Pérez (far right) performs a ritual greeting to open this *congreso* with the *saylas,* or chiefs, from other islands.

Molas and Tourism

Some Kuna grandmothers may recall when no one sold *molas.* It was not necessary. The land, animals, and sea provided everything they needed. However, changes in the Kuna economy began to make the sale of *molas* important. When Peace Corps volunteers came to the San Blas Islands in the 1960s, they helped organize the beginning of a **cooperative** of Kuna women. It was the women themselves who turned the idea into a full-fledged cooperative. Today the group has over 1,500 artisans. The women use the Internet, fax, and email to run their cooperative and sell their crafts.

A Good-Luck *Mola*

One Kuna mother made her fourteen-year-old daughter a special farewell *mola* when she left to go to school in Panama City. It showed an airplane within the open wings of a large bird to wish her daughter a safe trip.

Kuna Beliefs and Body Painting

The Kuna practiced body painting for centuries. They believe that every creature and plant has a spirit, and that the world is full of good and evil spirits.

The Development of *Mola* Designs

Original *mola* designs probably came from early forms of body decoration. The colors in body painting were red, yellow, black, and blue—colors now seen in *molas*.

▲ Young Kuna women wear colorful clothing. They wrap their wrists and ankles with bands of colored beads. They may wear rings and other jewelry.

Although *molas* are now worn in place of more intricate body painting, many women still paint the traditional thin black line on their noses. The dye is made from the juice of the sabdur tree, the Kuna's sacred Tree of Life. Kuna healers steep crushed leaves from this tree in water to make a solution to bathe the eyes of women who want to make beautiful *molas*.

The importance of *mola*-making is reflected even in the Kuna's spiritual beliefs in an afterlife. The Kuna believe that special houses exist in heaven for important members of the community. One house in heaven is reserved for artists.

◄ These children are proud to show visitors the beautiful *molas* made by women in their village.

Layers of Color

Molas are created using several techniques, or methods, including *reverse appliqué*. Several layers of brightly colored cloth (usually red, yellow, and blue) are laid on a backing. A design may be drawn on the top piece. Slits are cut and the edges turned under to reveal different colors and designs in the layers below. Final details are added with embroidery or appliqué.

Making *Molas*

Kuna women have made *molas* for about a century. It is one of the few cultures in which the pictorial art of the society is created only by women. Most Kuna girls learn to sew *molas* at age four or five from their mothers, aunts, or other women in their families. They begin by learning to make *pachis,* or *mola* patches, small squares with a design in the middle.

Mola Design

Each *mola* is a true work of art and may take several months to produce. *Mola*-makers never duplicate a design in a *mola*. If a *mola* has six frogs, each one will be different. Some basic design **motifs** are used by many *mola*-makers. Especially popular designs are copied and seen throughout the San Blas Islands. It is a great honor to have one's design copied by other *mola*-makers.

Mola Objects

Kuna women now use technology to make *mola* objects for sale to outsiders. These objects include children's toys, stuffed animals, children's clothes, and hats.

▲ The rich variety of animals in Panama inspire many *mola* designs.

◀ The Kuna Indians' peaceful island environment leaves plenty of time for creative *mola*-making.

Tools

- pencil
- width gauge—a strip of cardboard cut to 3/8-in. by 2 in. (1 by 3 cm)
- fabric scissors
- small embroidery scissors
- pins
- embroidery or quilting needles

Materials

- paper
- small pieces of colored paper (optional)
- dressmaker's transfer paper
- lightweight cotton fabrics in solid colors
- matching threads
- embroidery floss

Make a mola patch to put on your jacket or sew one onto a pillowcase.

Plan a *Mola* Patch

1. Sewing a *mola* patch takes some time and effort. For your first *mola* project, choose a simple image that you especially like. Think of your favorite plants, animals, and belongings. Look at patterns and geometric designs on objects. The Kuna Indians find ideas for *molas* almost anywhere!

2. Carefully select the fabric colors you will use for your patch. The top fabric is the main image and background. The bottom fabric is the strip, or channel, that surrounds and outlines the main image. *(See diagram.)*

3. Some *molas* use only two colors. Many, however, have colorful little shapes that fill the spaces around the main image. These filler shapes are made with small scraps of fabric. Filler shapes make *molas* lively and rich designs. *(See diagram.)*

4. Embroidered decoration is often added, using a simple *running stitch* and embroidery floss. Sometimes decorative stitches inside the main image are details, like feather designs on a bird or scales on a lizard. *(See diagram.)*

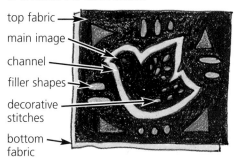

Plan a *Mola* Patch

2-4. Select the fabric colors.

- top fabric
- main image
- channel
- filler shapes
- decorative stitches
- bottom fabric

Helpful Hints

- The top fabric layer should be dark enough to hide the color underneath. Red or black are the most common choices, but you can use any dark color.

- The bottom fabric layer should be a color that strongly contrasts with the top fabric. This will help the design image to stand out from the background.

- The filler shapes are made of brightly colored fabric scraps that are arranged to create an eye-catching rhythm and pattern.

- Test your design and color choices using colored papers. Check to see that the design looks balanced and interesting.

Sewing a *mola* ▶ takes patience, but it is very rewarding.

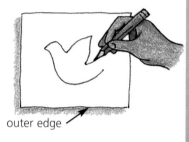

Draw the Pattern

1. Draw a basic pencil outline of your main design image in the center of a piece of white paper. Draw the image the size you want it to be on your patch. Five or six inches (about 15 cm) is a good size to start with. Make each outer edge of your patch nine or ten inches (about 25 cm). *(See diagram.)*

2. Draw a channel 3/8-inch (1 cm) or wider around your image. Use the cardboard width gauge to help you keep the channel the same width all the way around. *(See diagram.)*

3. Add filler shapes around your image if you wish. The most common filler shapes are triangles and slits, because they are easiest to sew. Straight edges are a little easier to sew than curves. *(See diagram.)*

4. Draw dotted pencil lines on your pattern to show where the decorative stitches will be. *(See diagram.)*

5. Now prepare the top and bottom fabrics. Use your pattern to measure the outer edges on the fabrics. Add an extra one-half inch (1.2 cm) on all sides so that you can turn under the raw edges later. Cut both pieces of fabric to the same size.

6. Copy the whole pattern on to the top fabric, using dressmaker's transfer paper. Sandwich the transfer paper, waxy side down, between the pattern and the fabric. Trace over the design. *(See diagram.)*

Draw the Pattern

1. Draw the main design image.

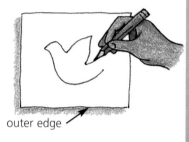

outer edge

2. Draw the channel.

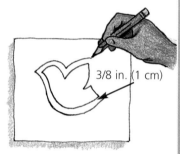

3/8 in. (1 cm)

3-4. Add filler shapes and decorative stitches.

Stitches You Will Use

Thread a needle and tie a knot at the end of the thread. You may use a single or double thread. Start sewing from the back of the bottom fabric so that the knot will be hidden.

running stitch – Sew in and out of the fabric in a straight line. Make stitches that are even in length.

tack stitch – Poke the needle up through the bottom fabric into the edge of the fold. Take a tiny stitch over the edge of the fold. Pull the thread tight. Repeat.

running stitch

tack stitch

6. Copy the pattern.

paper pattern

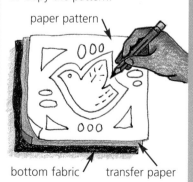

bottom fabric   transfer paper

Sew the Patch

2. Cut the main image.

3. Clip curved edges.

4. Sew around the main image.

tack stitch

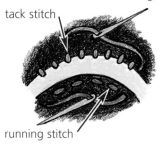

running stitch

5. Sew the filler shapes.

6. Add decorative stitches.

Sew the Patch

1. Put the top fabric in place over the bottom fabric. Pin the fabrics together at the four corners.

2. Begin to cut the main image through the top layer only. The cutting line is along the very center of the channel. Poke the embroidery scissors into the top fabric and snip a short section. *(See diagram.)*

3. Clip curved edges in to the fold line. This will help them to turn under smoothly. Fold the edges under on both sides of the channel. Press the folded edges flat with your finger. *(See diagram.)*

4. Thread two needles with thread that matches the top fabric. Sew down the first short section using a *tack stitch* or a *running stitch*. Use a different needle for each side of the channel. Continue sewing around the main image. Snip a little at a time and stitch it down on both sides. *(See diagram.)*

5. When you finish sewing the main image, you are ready to sew the filler shapes. Collect the scraps you will use. Arrange them on the top fabric to cover the filler shape outlines. Pin the scraps to the fabric. Clip and fold the edges under as you did for the main image. Sew the filler shapes down using a *tack stitch* or a *running stitch*. Remove the pins. *(See diagram.)*

6. Add the decorative stitches with embroidery floss, using a *running stitch. (See diagram.)*

7. Iron your *mola* patch. Fold the outside edges under and attach it to a jacket or a pillowcase.

Students' finished ▶
mola patches.

Other Ideas

■ For an easier *mola* patch, try using colorful pieces of felt. In this case, the edges will not need to be turned under.

GULF OF
MEXICO

MEXICO

Guatemalan artisans
make colorful wooden
animals to sell to tourists.

Tikal
National Park ▲

GUATEMALA

Petén Jungle

BELIZE

CARIBBEAN
SEA

Descendants of early Mayan
people live in the highland
village of Chichicastenango.

Gulf of
Honduras

Chixoy River

Lake
Izabal

Highland Region

Motagua River

HONDURAS

Tajumulco
Volcano

Chichicastenango

Quetzaltenango

Lake
Atitlán

Antigua

Guatemala
City

EL SALVADOR

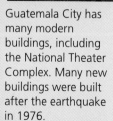

Guatemala City has
many modern
buildings, including
the National Theater
Complex. Many new
buildings were built
after the earthquake
in 1976.

Beautiful Lake Atitlán was
probably formed long ago
when volcanic ash blocked
an ancient valley.

PACIFIC
OCEAN

N
W E
S

0   75 miles
0   100 km

Guatemala

▲ Indian artisans travel from many villages to sell their products and crafts in Chichicastenango.

Guatemala Facts

Name: Republic of Guatemala (República de Guatemala) "The Land of Eternal Spring"
Capital: Guatemala City
Borders: Mexico, Belize, Honduras, El Salvador
Population: 11.5 million people; almost one-half native Indian people
Language: Official language: Spanish; 23 Indian languages
Size: Third largest country in Central America; 42,042 sq. mi. (108,889 sq km)
High/Low Point: Tajumulco volcano: 13,845 ft. (4,220 m); sea level along coast
Climate: Tropical; year-round daytime temperatures of 75° F (24° C); cooler nights of 40-50° F (3-7° C); dry season: November-May; rainy season: May-October
Wildlife: More than 800 kinds of mammals, birds, amphibians, and reptiles
Plants: 8,000 different kinds of plants

Market Day in Chichicastenango

It is Saturday evening in Chichicastenango. The highland village is filled with activity. People arrive with crafts and produce to sell at the market on Sunday morning. All along the windy mountain roads, local Indian artisans walk toward the village. Some carry weavings and other crafts. Farmers bring their fruits and vegetables. They come long distances to sell their goods and purchase things their families need.

In Chichicastenango's main square, the merchants unload their wares. They recognize friends from other villages by the ancient designs and colors of their traditional clothing. In the plaza **alcoves,** people talk together in native Mayan languages. The square is alive with families cooking supper and arranging their bedding for sleeping outside.

Before dawn, the men set up market stalls. They hang colorful woven cloth and pile the stalls with goods for sale. Women spread blankets and place their weavings on the ground. They set up their looms to weave during the day as they **barter** with customers. By mid-morning, the tourist buses arrive from Guatemala City. Sounds of buying and selling ring out in the square.

The market closes in late afternoon. Then the villagers join in the weekly religious ceremonies at Igelsia de Santo Tomás, where a Roman Catholic mass is combined with ancient Mayan ceremonies. By evening, market day is over. Chichicastenango is once again a quiet village in Guatemala's highlands.

◄ At the Sunday market in Chichicastenango's main square, Mayan people wearing traditional clothing sell food, crafts, and other items to villagers and tourists.

▲ Old and new ways often exist side by side in Guatemala.

A Land of Contrasts

In its modern cities, well-to-do Guatemalans of Spanish heritage run the affairs of the country. The capital, Guatemala City, is a busy urban center with high-rise offices, luxury hotels, shopping centers, and theaters. People wear modern clothing that comes mostly from the United States. Urban Guatemalans work hard to prosper and achieve personal success.

In Guatemalan villages like Chichicastenango, life has changed little over the centuries. There are narrow cobblestone streets and houses with red-tiled roofs. Many villages do not have electricity. People work long hours every day to take care of their crops and animals, carry firewood, cook, and care for the children. Some villagers work far away from home to earn money in factories or by picking crops on Guatemala's large plantations. They continue to practice the Mayan values of respect for nature and duty to the community. It is a world that seems very isolated from the rest of Guatemala.

The Mayan Civilization

Every Guatemalan village has stories that began over 1,000 years ago in the Mayan Civilization. The Mayans built more than 200 cities in Mexico, Guatemala, and other parts of Central America. During the Mayan Golden Age (A.D. 250 - 900), they developed an advanced culture centered in the Petén jungle of northern Guatemala. A visit to Tikal National Park will reveal the ruins of ancient Mayan pyramids, palaces, temples, markets, and shrines.

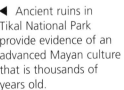

◀ Ancient ruins in Tikal National Park provide evidence of an advanced Mayan culture that is thousands of years old.

Mayan Achievements

- Observed and recorded the movements of the heavens
- Predicted solar and lunar eclipses
- Invented the concept of zero
- Recorded their history in hieroglyphs, a written, mainly picture language
- Developed an accurate yearly solar calendar of 365.2 days
- Built pyramids, temples, and aqueducts without metal tools, wheels, or pack animals
- Developed farming techniques that are still used today
- Played ball games
- Took steam baths to cleanse their souls and bodies

The Mayan goddess Ixchel was considered the goddess of weaving. Today, village weavers honor Ixchel. They also use the simple backstrap loom used by Mayan artisans.

TIMELINE

1500 B.C.	A.D. 900-1524	1839	1930	1998
Start of Mayan civilization in Guatemala.	Decline of Mayan civilization.	Guatemala becomes a republic.	Strong trade with the United States; banana boom begins.	Hurricane Mitch kills 258; 120 missing; and over 19,000 houses damaged or destroyed.

A.D. 250-900	1523-1540	1872	1976
Golden Age of Mayan civilization.	The Spanish, led by Pedro de Alvarado, conquer Guatemala.	Start of the coffee boom.	Earthquake kills 30,000; 20 percent of the people left homeless.

Mayan legend predicted the coming of the Spanish:

"Men who are clothed, not naked like thee, well armed; men who are cruel will arrive tomorrow or the next day. These will destroy your monuments, which will become the home of the wild fowl and mountain lions. The grandeur of this Court will cease to be."

▲ Indian village weavers use backstrap looms to weave colorful clothing with traditional patterns.

Spanish Impact on Weaving

- Use of wool
- Decorative floral styles
- Style of clothing, such as men's pants
- Treadle loom
- Spinning wheel

The Spanish Conquest

In 1502, Christopher Columbus's teenage son wrote that his father's ship had come upon a giant tree-trunk canoe loaded with goods. The Mayan boat held colorful woven cloth and other supplies. This discovery convinced the Spaniards that they had come upon a prosperous trade route. They seized the cargo and the boat's leader. By 1522, a Spanish officer, Pedro de Alvarado, invaded Guatemala with troops, guns, and horses. His plan was to get rich and "bring light to those in darkness." Within two years, the Spanish had conquered most of Central America.

The majority of Mayans died in battle or from Spanish-introduced diseases. Some Mayans escaped to the mountains and continued to fight. The Spanish government burned most of their writings. The Mayans were forced to practice Catholicism instead of their native religion. In every way, the Mayans and their descendants were treated as less than human.

Spanish Influence

Village weavers learned about new materials, techniques, and styles from the Spanish. Male weavers use the Spanish treadle loom to make larger items, such as blankets and shawls. However, village women still use the Mayan backstrap loom. This loom is made of pieces of dry wood. A strap is tied around the waist of the weaver, while the other end of the loom is attached to a tree branch. Tension is controlled by the movement forward or backward of the weaver's body. Their use of the backstrap loom, along with traditional colors, patterns, and styles of clothing, is evidence of their **resistance** to their Spanish conquerors.

A Land of Highland Weavers

Guatemala's highlands stretch from the city of Antigua to the Mexican border. To reach highland villages like Chichicastenango, one travels through valleys, pine forests, and mountains. Everywhere, small cottages are surrounded by fields of *maíz,* or corn. These are the traditional *milpas,* or farms, of the highland people.

Village Life and Identity

A person's clothing tells which village she or he comes from. Village weavers use their skills and creativity to reproduce the symbols that are special to each village. Colors, **motifs,** and patterns provide information about a person's work, family, and position. In Chichicastenango, the design of a man's traditional clothing tells if he is married, the number of children he has, and how many sons are married. These identifying patterns in men's clothing are used mostly for ceremonial purposes. The women, however, take great pride in weaving and wearing their traditional village clothing.

A Weaving Tradition

In a country shaken by volcanoes, earthquakes, armed conflicts, and poverty, the weavers preserve tradition and village identity and earn much-needed money. They keep alive a sense of community that the Mayans believe is a person's first duty. On village festival days, wearing traditional clothing is an act of great pride.

Traditional Clothing

tzute
head cloth

faja
waist sash

huipil
blouse

◀ Village men wear clothing woven on a backstrap loom.

Weaving Schools

Tourists can attend *La Escuela de Tejer,* a special school in the town of Quetzaltenango. There, they will learn to weave from master weavers in cooperatives that market weavers' creations.

Materials and Tools

Weavers use Guatemalan-produced cotton, wool, silk, and vegetable fiber for weaving. Traditionally, fibers were spun into yarn and colored with natural dyes from plants, trees, roots, and other living things. Today, yarn is often factory-produced. These **acrylic yarns** come in brilliant colors that do not fade easily like yarns colored with natural dyes.

Natural Dyes

Indigo blue	indigo plant
Red	cochineal or achiote plant
Brown	bark of the nance tree
Green	liquid of the curcuma root
Yellow	iron hydroxide or blackberry tree
Violet	extract from mollusk, *Purpura patula*

Violet is the most-prized color. It is used on *huipiles* worn on religious holidays.

The Weaving Community

Most of the weaving in the village is done by women. Between household and childcare duties, the women sit and weave together on backstrap looms. Because these looms are inexpensive and very portable, the women can weave almost anywhere, inside or outside of the house. Using this simple handloom, they produce beautiful, complex designs that are a combination of traditional patterns and their own artistic ideas. Their *huipiles*, or blouses, are examples of their extraordinary skill and artistry.

Everyone in the family helps weave clothing for family use, or to sell at the market or through a weavers' cooperative. Boys learn how to use a floor loom from their fathers. From the age of six, girls work beside their mothers and learn to weave on backstrap looms. Weaving skill is a Mayan woman's greatest source of pride. A young girl usually owns a loom that she will have all her life and which will be buried with her. She cannot hope to marry well unless she can weave. A girl will offer her first *huipil* to a Catholic saint, just as her ancestors did to the Mayan goddess Ixchel.

◄ Backstrap weavers work together in the village. They teach their skills to their daughters.

Weaving Colors From Nature

Guatemalan weavers are influenced by colors of nature they see all around them, such as the yellows, reds, browns, and blacks of the corn they grow. The beautiful colors in the sacred quetzal bird has inspired Mayan weavers for centuries. Its long, trailing tail feathers were used to decorate the head-dresses of Mayan leaders. Today, they decorate traditional clothing in festivals and religious ceremonies.

Ancient Symbols and Patterns

Many Guatemalan weavers' symbols come from ancient religious traditions that use animal images and geometric patterns. Images of animals, such as the deer, jaguar, snake, and monkey, are used in many ways. Sometimes, like their Mayan ancestors, weavers combine more than one animal. They weave two-headed creations like the snake-bird or jaguar-eagle.

Modern weavers continue to weave symbols of the sun, the moon, and the stars. Their patterns trace the paths these heavenly bodies take across the sky. Kak, the Mayan god of lightning, is honored in repeated lightning bolts or chevron patterns. Geometric forms are often combined to represent the four directions: north, south, east, and west.

New Trends

- Factory-made clothing, yarns, and dyes are used.
- Armed conflicts have taken away many men from the villages.
- Women have less time for weaving.
- Young people leave the villages to work in cities.
- Tourists desire nontraditional patterns.

Symbols

swan
water

two-headed eagle
struggle between
good and evil

mountain cat
love of the sun
and the moon

Tools

- colored pencils

- backstrap loom or small frame loom. Frame looms can be purchased at art or weaving stores. To make a backstrap loom, refer to the books listed in the Resources on page 47.

- several shuttles (ice-cream sticks or strips of strong cardboard)

- wooden ruler

- scissors

Materials

- background weaving yarn, 8/4 cotton carpet warp for the warp and weft. A large spool has 800 yards (731 m), enough for four pouches. You can find it at any store that sells yarn.

- pattern yarns, 3/2 pearl cotton or other yarns that are about twice as thick as the background yarn. You will need about 3 to 4 feet (1-1.2 m) of each color.

- graph paper

Are you ready for a challenge? Once you learn how to use a loom, you will be amazed by the beautiful weavings you can create in a short time! Begin by collecting the tools and materials you will need.

Weaving Terms

backstrap— the belt that wraps around the weaver's back and attaches to the bottom beam of a backstrap loom

batten— a smooth, flat piece of wood used to hold open the shed and push down each row of weft yarn used in weaving

beams— the top and bottom sticks on a backstrap loom

rod heddle— one of the two parts of a loom that are used to change the shed and separate the top and bottom layers of the warp yarn loop

shed— the space between the top and bottom layers of the warp yarn loop

shuttle— a tool that holds the yarn for weaving

string heddle— one of the two parts of a loom that are used to change the shed and separate the top and bottom layers of the warp yarn loop

warp yarn— the foundation yarn that stretches from the top beam to the bottom beam of the loom in a big loop

weft yarn— yarn that is woven back and forth across the warp

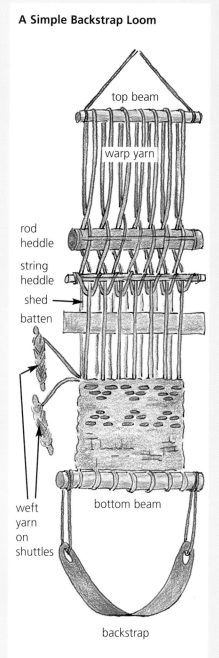

A Simple Backstrap Loom

top beam

warp yarn

rod heddle

string heddle

shed

batten

weft yarn on shuttles

bottom beam

backstrap

Prepare to Weave

You can weave a pouch with a small frame loom, or you can build a simple backstrap loom similar to those used in Guatemala. In either case, setting up a loom for the first time is challenging. **Find someone with experience to help you.**

To make a pouch, you will weave a flat piece of fabric on the loom. Then you will fold your woven fabric in half and sew up the sides to form the pouch.

1. First, plan the size of your pouch. Draw the shape of the front of your pouch on graph paper. Make it no more than eight inches (20 cm) wide. Draw the back of the pouch just below it. Add one-half inch (1.3 cm) for a hem at each end. *(See diagram.)*

2. Choose the yarn colors. In Guatemala, the background weaving yarn is often red or blue. The pattern yarns are very bright. You may choose to follow this same approach, or you may select other colors.

3. Now you are ready to put the warp yarn on the loom and attach the heddles. Refer to one of the books listed on page 47 for detailed instructions. **Ask an adult to help you.**

4. When the loom is ready, wrap a shuttle with about three feet (1 m) of your background weaving yarn, the same yarn used for the warp. This is the weft yarn. You will also need a batten, such as a wooden ruler.

5. Tie the top beam of your backstrap loom to a heavy table leg or a tree trunk. Stretch the warp out on the ground.

6. Make yourself comfortable on a chair or pillow. Lift the bottom beam onto your lap, and wrap the backstrap around your back. Tie the backstrap to the other side of the bottom beam. Adjust the loom so that it is straight and the strings are taut. Push the rod heddle up toward the top beam. You are ready to weave! *(See diagram.)*

A friendly gathering of weavers. ▶

Note!

The looms illustrated on these pages show only a small number of warp yarns in order to make the process easier to see and understand. An actual loom for a pouch may have 120 complete warp loops, or 240 warp yarns all together, top and bottom.

Prepare To Weave

1. Plan the size of your pouch.

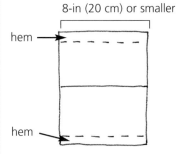
8-in (20 cm) or smaller
hem →
hem →

6. Ready to weave.

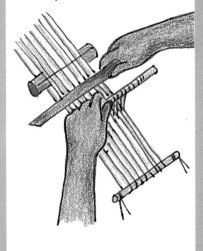

The Background Weave

1. Pull the string heddle up.

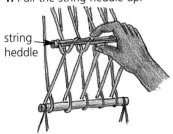

string heddle

2. Insert the batten in the shed.

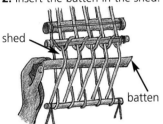

shed

batten

3. Leave a loose arc of weft yarn.

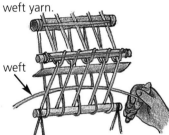

weft

4. Push the weft yarn down.

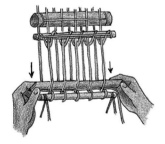

5. Pull the rod heddle down.

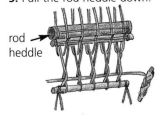

rod heddle

The Background Weave

1. Pull the string heddle up firmly but smoothly. (If you jerk the heddle, the warp yarns may break.) All the bottom warp yarns will move above the top warp yarns. *(See diagram.)*

2. The space that is created between the top and bottom warp yarns is called the shed. Insert the batten in the shed. Stand the batten on its side in order to hold the shed open. *(See diagram.)*

3. Slip the shuttle with the weft yarn into the shed in front of the batten. Slide the shuttle out the other side, leaving a loose arc of weft yarn. *(See diagram.)*

4. With the edge of the batten, firmly push the weft down toward the bottom beam. Remove the batten. *(See diagram.)*

5. Now change sheds. To do this, pull the rod heddle down toward you. The warp yarns will close over the weft yarn, and a new shed will form. *(See diagram.)*

6. Insert the batten in front of the rod heddle. Stand the batten on its side. Slip the weft shuttle back through the shed in the opposite direction. Push the weft down again with the batten. *(See diagram.)*

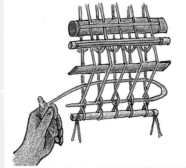

6. Weave in the other direction.

7. Continue weaving a small strip of background weave. This strip will be one of the top edges of your pouch. When you are ready for a break, release the backstrap and carefully roll the loom up. Store it in a safe place where the strings will not get tangled.

Weaving Hints

■ To keep the edges of your weaving even, remember to apply the weft in a loose arc. The arc allows some give, so that the edges of your pouch will not get narrower as you weave.

■ Change the tension of the warp yarns as you weave by leaning forward or backward. Keep the tension, or pressure, looser when you are using the string heddle.

■ Guatemalan weaving is warp-faced. This means that the warp yarns are very close together, almost completely covering the weft yarns.

Brocade Pattern Weave

A brocade pattern is a raised design that lies on top of the background weave. It is a common way to decorate fabric in Guatemala. This pattern is made with an extra weft of thicker yarn. Make a simple brocade pattern to decorate your pouch.

1. Open a shed and weave one row of background weft. Push it down with the batten. Leave the shed open.

2. Wrap about one foot (30 cm) of pattern weft yarn onto a shuttle. Choose a color that will stand out against your background weave.

3. Slip this shuttle into the shed from the same side as the background weft. Go only a short way, under about four warp yarns. This part of the pattern weft stays inside the shed with the background weft. Now, poke the shuttle up toward yourself, and pull it out between the warp yarns. *(See diagram.)*

4. Stretch the pattern weft over the top of the next two warp yarns. Then put the shuttle back into the shed. This part of the weft floats on top of the warp and makes the pattern that you will see. *(See diagram.)*

5. Continue across the row, weaving under four warp yarns and over two. End the row by going under a few warp yarns. Push the pattern weft down with the batten. This first row of the pattern will look like a row of dotted lines. *(See diagram.)*

6. For the second row, change the shed and weave in the other direction. Weave a row of background weft, followed by a row of pattern weft. This time, weave the pattern weft over and under a different set of warp yarns. *(See diagram.)*

Pattern Hints

■ Brocade patterns are usually geometric, because making rounded shapes is hard to do on a loom.

■ Don't try to stretch the pattern weft over more than ten warp yarns. It will be too loose.

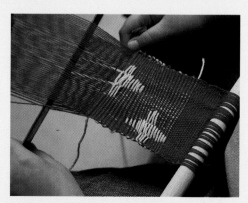

▲ Carrie has designed a flower brocade pattern.

Brocade Pattern Weave

3. Pull the shuttle out between the warp yarns.

4. Stretch the pattern weft over two warp yarns.

pattern weft

background weft

5. Weave under four, over two.

6. Weave a second row of pattern.

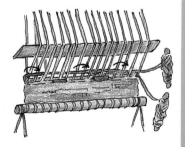

7. Design a pattern on graph paper.

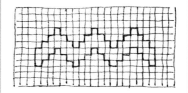

Finish Your Pouch

1. Cut the warp yarns.

2. Sew your pouch.

hem

sides

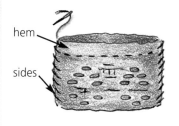

Other Ideas

■ Use a thicker yarn for the background, such as 3/2 pearl cotton.

■ Weave a narrow band for a belt or a bookmark.

7. You can continue to make up a pattern as you go. You can also plan out a pattern on graph paper with colored pencils. Look at Guatemalan weaving patterns for ideas. *(See diagram.)*

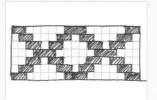

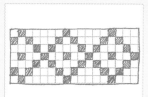

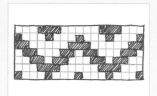

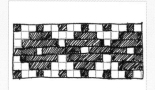

Guatemalan brocade designs

Finish Your Pouch

1. When you have finished weaving your pouch, cut the warp yarns across the top and bottom. Take off the two heddles and beams. *(See diagram.)*

2. Fold the edges under and sew a hem at the top and bottom. Then fold the weaving in half and sew the sides together. You can add a closing device, such as a drawstring or a button, if you like. *(See diagram.)*

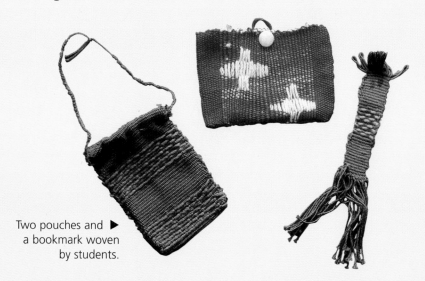

Two pouches and ▶
a bookmark woven
by students.

45

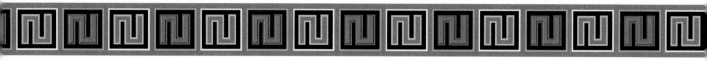

Glossary

acrylic yarns quick-drying synthetic yarns; not a natural fiber, such as wool

alcoves arched openings as in a wall

archipelago a group of islands

artisans people who are skilled in an art, a craft, or a trade

assimilation becoming absorbed into the culture of a population or group

barter to trade or exchange for needed goods

colonial relating to land ruled by another country

consensus an agreement reached by a group

cooperative a group formed in order to effectively produce and market products, such as handicrafts

dictator a ruler who has complete power over the people

exploited taken advantage of; used for one's own advantage

extended family other family members in addition to parents and children

isthmus a narrow strip of land connecting two larger land areas

machete a large, heavy knife used for cutting underbrush

mestizo a person with both Native American and European ancestors

motif a repeated design or theme in a work of art

oppression excessive use of authority or power

plateau a level land surface raised sharply above land next to it on at least one side

resistance the act of opposing or fighting back

stilts two poles, each with a footrest, used to raise the person wearing them high above the ground when walking

Abbreviations Key

C	Centigrade
cm	centimeters
F	Fahrenheit
ft.	feet
g	grams
in.	inches
km	kilometers
m	meters
mi.	miles
sq.	square

Resources

Mexico

Atkin, Beth. *Faces from the Fields.* Boston, MA: Little Brown, 1993

Box, Ben, ed. *Mexico and Central America Handbook 1994.* Lincolnwood, IL: Passport Books, 1993

Fisher, Leonard Everett. *Pyramid of the Sun, Pyramid of the Moon.* New York: Macmillan, 1985

Kalman, Bobbie. *Mexico—the Land,* "Lands, Peoples, and Cultures" series. New York: Crabtree, 1993

Lewington, Anna. *Mexico: Study of an Economically Developing Country.* Austin, TX: Raintree Steck-Vaughn, 1996

Morrison, Marion. *Mexico and Central America,* "Places and People" series. New York: Watts, 1995

Nicaragua

Brosnahan, Tom, et. al. *Central America: A Lonely Planet Shoestring Guide* (2nd ed.). Oakland, CA: Lonely Planet, 1994

Griffiths, John. *Nicaragua,* "Major World Nations" series. Broomall, PA: Chelsea House, 1998

Haverstock, Nathan A. *Nicaragua in Pictures,* "Visual Geography" series. Minneapolis, MN: Lerner, 1993

Malone, Michael. *A Nicaraguan Family,* "Journey Between Two Worlds" series. Minneapolis, MN: Lerner, 1998

The Puppeteers' Cooperative Home Page: 68 Ways to Make Really Big Puppets.
http://www.gis.net/~puppetco/index.html

Panama

Doggett, Scott. *Panama*. Oakland, CA: Lonely Planet, 1999

Parker, Ann. *Molas, Folk Art of the Cuna Indian*. Barre, MA: Barre, 1997

Patera, Charlotte. *Mola Techniques for Today's Quilters*. American Quilter's Society (PO Box 3290, Paducah, KY 42002-3290), 1995

Presilla, Maricel E. *Mola: Cuna Life, Stories, and Art*. New York: Holt, 1995

Schlesinger, Arthur Meier, ed. *Building the Panama Canal: Chronicles from National Geographic*. Broomall, PA: Chelsea House, 1999

Guatemala

Bjerregaard, Lena. *Techniques of Guatemalan Weaving*. New York: Van Nostrand Reinhold, 1977

Black, Nancy J., and Mary Turck. *Guatemala: Land of the Maya*, "Discovering Our Heritage" series. New York: Dillon Silver Burdett, 1998

Box, Ben, ed. *Mexico and Central America Handbook 1994*. Lincolnwood, IL: Passport Books, 1993

Haynes, Tricia. *Guatemala*, "Major World Nations" series. Broomall, PA: Chelsea House, 1998

Lerner Publications, Department of Geography Staff. *Guatemala in Pictures*, rev. ed., "Visual Geography" series. Minneapolis, MN: Lerner, 1997

Sperlich, Norbert, and Elizabeth Katz Sperlich. *Guatemalan Backstrap Weaving*. Norman: University of Oklahoma Press, 1980

Index

Acknowledgments

Special thanks to these students for their time and energy in making the project samples: Aisha, Anna, Breeze, Carrie B., Carrie S., Eleanor, Jessica, Laurel, Samantha, and Quail; and to Danny, Lok, Maurice, Sarah, and Tyler for their help. Thanks also to Jefferson Middle School, Eugene, Oregon; Christie Newland; Sara Peattie; Marilyn Robert; Diane Cissell, Terragraphics; CHOICE Humanitarian/Salt Lake City; Mari Lyn Salvador, University of New Mexico; Libris Solar; Percy Franklin; Wade Long; Carol Shelton; City Copy; and the wonderful reference librarians at the Eugene Public Library and Salt Lake City Public Library.